# Daily Prophetic Prayers

Best Meditations

Written by Caroline Phillip
124 Rue des Bosquets
Sainte-Sophie, Québec
Canada, J5J 0H2

Date Deposited: 28 August 2022

Printed by Amazon Demand

ISBN: 9798848750089

## TABLE OF CONTENTS

## Daily Prophetic Prayers

1. I am grateful to you, Lord, for giving me life

2. Your mighty hands have sustained me, Father God.

3. I am grateful for the breath of life that you have given me.

4. Your grace and mercy have been of great help to me.

5. It has been a pleasure living under your protection.

6. My life was spared from death even in hard times because of your mercy.

7. Thank you, God, for being merciful to my family and loved ones.

8. You have provided me with a new season to enjoy; thank you, O' Lord.

9. There is a supernatural power at work in me during this season of manifestation.

10. I declare and decree today that all the promises made by God for me will come to pass in Jesus' name.

11. By the power of Jesus, I decree and declare that everything I say will become a reality in my life.

12. I am who God says I am, I possess what God says I will possess, and I am able to accomplish what God says I can accomplish, in Jesus' name.

13.As I place my faith in Jesus, every opposition to my God-given gift must be removed.

14. All obstacles to the manifestation of my peace now fall and catch fire, in the name of Jesus.

15. I decree and declare that every prophetic word in my life will come to pass.

16. I put my faith in Jesus, and I am able to do what God says.

17. Whatever is done in the open or in secret to destroy my blessing, must catch fire, in the name of Jesus.

18. Whoever stands against me will be opposed, in the name of Jesus.

19. My life will not be dominated by anyone serving the interests of evil

20. Every saucier spirit attacking my life must fall now, In Jesus' name.

21. Any witch fighting my finance must fall now, in Jesus' Name.

22. Every wizard spirit attacking my life must fall now, in Jesus' name.

23. I take authority over every assigned devil working to steal my miracle, in the name of Jesus.

24. Every satanic alter erected against life be demolished now, in the name of Jesus.

25. I disassociate myself from every bloodline spirit operating in my life, in Jesus' name.

26. I disassociate myself from every bloodline curse operating in my life, in Jesus' name.

27. Through God's grace, I renounce all ungodly covenants I have either knowingly or unknowingly entered into which are used by the enemy to harm me.

28. Every satanic alter erected against me will be demolished, in the name of Jesus.

29. I disassociate myself from every bloodline curse operating in my life, in Jesus' name.

30. Through God's grace, I renounce all ungodly covenants I have either knowingly or unknowingly entered into which are used by the enemy to harm me.

31. I plead the blood of Jesus over life. I decree and declare that every door to every false spirit in my life is closed and sealed, in the name of Jesus.

32. In the name of Jesus, I command all wizards and witches fighting against me in the spiritual realm to dry up and catch fire right now.

33. In the name of Jesus, I condemn every tongue speaking against me.

34. I break every spell of lust in my life, in the name of Jesus.

35. May every wizard who speaks against my property be punished, in the name of Jesus.

36. I will not fall, I will rise up, in Jesus' name.

37. I will keep on moving forward, in Jesus' name.

38. In the name of Jesus, those who seek my life will be scattered in 7 directions.

39. I command every lock door of favor to open now, in the name of Jesus.

40. My enemies will flood me with their attacks, but the spirit of God will lift me up.

41. In the name of Jesus, I will see the back of my enemies, as they run away from me.

42. I declare and decree I am a child of God, and I will not die before time, in the name of Jesus.

43. No charm from the wicked can stop me, in Jesus' name.

44. I decree and declare, in Jesus' name, that I am unstoppable.

45. The God I serve makes me invisible, to all my enemies.

46. I am strengthened by Jesus Christ who enables me to accomplish all things.

47. I am blessed, I am not cursed

48. The blessing of Abraham belongs to me, in the name of Jesus.

49.There will be no bad news in my home, in the name of Jesus.

50. In the name of Jesus, every evil that is planned against me will turn into a force that will work in my favor.

51. In the name of Jesus, there will be no hatred in my home.

52. Any opposition to my blessing must submit to the absolute will of the highest God.

53. I pray that my Lord and Savior Jesus Christ will grant me what is rightfully mine.

54. I declare and decree that I will not die before my time, that I will live long enough to see the wonderful things God has in store for me.

55. By the stripes of Jesus Christ I am healed, and saved.

56. No virus can survive in me, in the name of Jesus.

57. I demolish all illnesses and diseases in my family bloodline, in the name of Jesus.

58. Covid –19 is not my portion, in the mighty name of Jesus

59. My body is the temple of the holy spirit, and God loves me.

60. I cover myself with the blood of Jesus Christ, and no weapon formed against me will prosper.

61. All spirit of infirmity, I demand you to leave my body now, and never return, in the mighty name of Jesus.

62. The God who raised Jesus Christ from the dead also vitalize body now.

63. I declare divine strength in my body, in the name of Jesus.

64. I destroy every struggle in my life with the blood of Jesus Christ.

65. I will be the best person I can be, in the name of Jesus.

66. Gold and silver belongs to
the highest God so wealth is mine.

67. Every pit of financial problems trying to pull me down, I destroy your powers, in the name of Jesus.

68. I command doors of financial blessing to open up now, in the name of Jesus.

69. O' Father God, let your goodness and mercy follow me.

70. O' Lord, Let your grace, and presence manifest in my life, in the name of Jesus.

## THE POWER OF GOD

71. I decree and declare, that my feet are catching speed to succeed in everything I do, in the mighty name of Jesus.

72. My children and I shall always be number one in everything we do, in the name of Jesus.

73. I shall be the ahead not the tale, in the name of Jesus.

74. I Shall enter new grounds of financial projects, in the name of Jesus.

75. My family shall not die before their time; they will testify the Goodness of God in the land of the living.

76, Whatever I desire I will receive it now, in the name of Jesus.

77. O' Father Lord God, honor me and answer my Cry for help.

78. I decree and declare; I take my rightful position in the spiritual realm and speak to the manifestation of blessing from God.

79. I belong to the Jesus Christ, and I dedicated my children and family into hands.

80. I connected myself to God' divine alter.

81. My alter is built on God' unfailing words.

82. Neither the devil nor his associates are stronger than my alter, so they can never, me defeated, in the name of Jesus.

83. In the mighty name of Jesus, I take back all of my possessions that were stolen by the enemy.

84. I decree and declare; I am I child of God.

85. I command the heavenly places to release every blessing that belongs to me now, in the mighty name of Jesus.

86. I command the ministering angels of my life to fulfill their Godly mission to help me now.

87. I decree and declare, that every evil seed planted in my yard is uprooted now, in the name of Jesus.

88. By the precious blood of Jesus Christ, I decree and declare that every word I pronounced in God in these prophetic prayers is sealed in my life. So, shall it be. It is done!

89. Declarations of faith I decree and declare that God exists, and he is able to do exceedingly and abundantly.

90. Above all that you ask and think according to the power at work within all things.

91. I decree and declare that besides God, there is no other powerful creator.

92. I declare all powers belongs to God.

93. When I contemplate your splendor, your greatness and the very way you fill this whole great surface of the earth, I say O God, everything is a quarter of a meter from your hands!

94. This is how you fill this world! O God how can I be away from you.

95.  Bless you be my father because the finesse and the miniature of your works which prove to be grandiose fills my heart with joy. I

96. will praise you my God because you are unique forever.

97. Through His resurrection, He redeemed us as priests from His father. Children of God confess faith in Jesus Christ and accept that you are god's true chosen people.

98. Because by his blood we have become the children of heaven. We are conquerors of this world by the name of God Jesus Christ.

98. Under our feet, they have all been subdued because we share the glory of Christ.

99. Ask and you will be given.

100. Love the Lord your God with all your heart, strength and soul and love your neighbor as yourself are the greatest of all commandments and preaching.

101. May the Lord give us the spirit and heart of God's children.

102. Do not ask the question to the one who is not in charge of helping you.

103. Find the strength and the taste to know by appreciating all that we can learn.

104. Find someone else to refer to. The Lord asks us to be persistent.

105. “For which of my works will you stone me?" the Lord Jesus Christ asked once in the synagogue. For which of your works do they want to stone today? so I ask you.

106. Believe me, no son of God is sinful or hidden from God's grace, for those who are of God do not sin but fulfill God's will.

107. Those who have received God's word as a tradition are different from those who have received it through the Holy Spirit.

108. For a tradition wears out over time, but those who have the Holy Spirit, have the living words of God in their hearts, bodies and souls.

109. This is the difference between sons of God and servants of God. For things have not been made perfect by God's servants rather by the one who is above all, his son.

110. The new covenant lies not only in God's scriptures but also in His own will to manifest himself in man (Emmanuel GOD among men).

111. As the Lord Jesus said: you have been told to hate your enemies according to the scriptures, but I tell you "love your enemies and pray for them".

112. By this gesture, the living word of God was manifested in man. Live the word of God by being alive and not in tradition.

113. Be victorious. Those who received the word of God as a tradition are like Pharisees and Sadducees who had the word of God but did not know how to determine the presence of Christ.

114. Because words (scriptures) may become obsolete in people's hearts as the seed falls on the rock.

115. Strength is spiritual as well as physical.

116. Don't miss the opportunity to be protected by the one who is above everything.

117. Demonstrate your sense of responsibility and enjoy the fullness of your freedom.

118. know that your actions can have both positive and negative effects in your life, and of those around you.

119. Count on the Lord to protect yourself from yourself and all that is happening in your life.

120. Simply confess in yourself that Jesus Christ is Lord and Savior of the souls of this world. You will see the result.

121. Make the necessary efforts to build a responsible image for yourself because your name is worth more than gold.

122. With a responsible name, one can be entrusted with higher tasks.

123. By the Name of Jesus Christ, we are saved. By the Name of God, we are protected.

## FAITH IN GOD

124. What is your name? God bless you.

125. Do not stop working and honor God with your thanks.

126. Always look at your life from a positive angle even if the world wants to show you the opposite.

127. Believe that they are not capable of it, meditate on your life and never forget to make a good reference of your past because no one is perfect.

128. God loves you and respects you so love who you are at all times. God bless you.

129. Man's strength comes from God. With all our mentalities.

130. Mentalities can only be changed with evidence. Only the evidence proves the truth in all its magnitudes.

131. If you want to change the mentality of the world, get proof.

132. If you want to, you can get involved.

133. Have ambition because ambition awakens ideas and ideas give us success.

134. Have ambition because it is a powerful force in man.

135. Don't forget it. God bless you. Life belongs to God and if in this life you are not better then forget your desire for paradise.

136. This world belongs to God and you will be judged for what you do in this world so that you can inherit paradise.

137. Faith is not only a force that allows us to affirm what you do not see and what you do not have.

138. Faith is also the strength to act, to work, to take important actions in the most desperate circumstances.

139. To be able to provide a solution even if you do not know the final results, only God provides.

140. Go work hard and smart because only God knows. God bless you.

141. The Spirit is greater than the physical, and the invisible God is Spirit.

142. The one who is invisible created the physical world.

143. Our World, my friends and brothers, is lifted up by spirits.

144. Be strong in spirit to be creators and workers: accomplished as our God.

145. For grace has be given us to be children of God. God bless you.

146. People will always try to get the wrong of you so they may feel better about themselves.

147. Watch out! Success comes from what you attach to your name.

148. What you can do for yourself despite the difficulties is believing in yourself and also believing in God.

149. Be strong and don't let go of your dreams. Be patient because the depth of life is more than what you can see.

150. Then possible or not. What do we know? Fire, water, hot or cold, true or false, listen you don't know so be courageous.

151. Something I know, I have always been victorious by God's grace and love and I had never lost a fight by his love.

152. I celebrate my life. Does it heat up at home? Or just a lack of tolerance.

153. And if you want to give up your life to defend the cause of the nation. Why say no to God.

154. I think that history does not give us enough wisdom rather a memory because everyone wants to try out.

155. What falls on the majority of the people whom in the end do not even know what they want?

156. Is democracy is the art of understanding, deciding, acting, and interpreting? I submit to you.

157. Love Life and Love God, He owns it all.

I thank all my followers and fans on the social media network. Thanks to you all for your love and time.

By working with you, I have collected the insight that helped me accomplish this book.

Thank my kids whose love is so huge.

Thanks to Jedelia Kabu Tshilombo and Arhielle Phillip Tshilombo my daughters.

Thank you for reading this material. For any questions please contact: phillipcaorline03@gmail.com, (PayPal) we will be happy to help. For your donation, feel free to help.

This book is the property of Caroline Phillip and views are strictly Caroline's. Thank you for your understanding.

www.ingramcontent.com/pod-product-compliance
Lightning Source LLC
LaVergne TN
LVHW020546160826
845677LV00015B/4230